# Tet
## Vietnamese New Year

### Dianne M. MacMillan

**Reading Consultant:**

Michael P. French, Ph.D.
Bowling Green State University

*—Best Holiday Books—*

ENSLOW PUBLISHERS, INC.

Bloy St. & Ramsey Ave.     P.O. Box 38
Box 777                               Aldershot
Hillside, N.J. 07205     Hants GU12 6BP
U.S.A.                                       U.K.

## Acknowledgments

*The author wishes to thank Ms. Thaveeporn Vasavakul for her careful review of the manuscript; and Hoang Vu Cuong, tutor of Vietnamese language at the World Language Institute, State University of New York, Buffalo, for his review of the Vietnamese language and pronunciations used in the text; and Thanh Thuy Le, a dedicated teacher who celebrates Tet with her students and community each year.*

**Library of Congress Cataloging-in-Publication Data**

MacMillan, Dianne.
    Tet: Vietnamese New Year / Dianne M. MacMillan.
      p. cm. — (Best holiday books)
    Includes index.
    ISBN 0-89490-501-5
    1. Vietnamese New Year—Juvenile literature. 2. Vietnamese New Year—
United States—Juvenile literature. 3. Vietnamese Americans—
Social life and customs—Juvenile literature. [1. Vietnamese New Year.
2. Vietnamese New Year—United States. 3. Vietnamese Americans—
Social life and customs.] I. Title. II. Series.
GT4905.M34  1994                              93-46184
394.2'61—dc20                             CIP
                                          AC

**Illustration Credits:** Bonnie Rhodes, p. 8; Dianne M. MacMillan, pp. 4, 6, 12, 14, 15, 17, 20, 21, 24, 28, 29, 32, 34, 36, 37, 39, 41; ©D.J. Lambrecht, p. 22; Priscilla Ton, p. 16.

**Cover Illustraton:** Charlott Nathan

# Contents

Boys and girls hurry inside the gate to celebrate Tet, the Vietnamese New Year.

# A Big Holiday

Boys and girls hurry through the gate. Over the park entrance hang banners with good wishes in Vietnamese. Pictures show people and scenes from Vietnam. Music is playing. Once inside the park, there will be special food and games. Booths will have things to buy. Parents look forward to meeting friends. Everyone is excited. All this fun takes place in the United States when Vietnamese Americans celebrate Tet. Tet is the Vietnamese New Year.

Vietnamese families have waited a whole year to celebrate. Tet is like a birthday, Thanksgiving, Christmas, and New Year's celebration all rolled into one holiday. It lasts for three days.

Tet marks the return of spring and the New Year. For over four thousand years, the Vietnamese have celebrated this holiday. Today Tet is celebrated wherever Vietnamese people live. In this book we will tell about the ways Tet is celebrated in the United States and Canada.

During Tet, Vietnamese Americans think about the past year and make plans for the coming year. It is a mixture of happiness, noise,

Booths will have things to buy at the Tet celebration in the park.

thanksgiving, and remembering. In the United States, it is a special time to learn about family history and the history of Vietnam. Everywhere it is a time for Vietnamese to be proud.

Vietnam is a small country in Southeast Asia. The country of
China is to the north. To the west of Vietnam are the countries of
Laos and Cambodia.

## How the Holiday Began

Many Vietnamese Americans were born in Vietnam. Vietnam is a small country in Southeast Asia. To the north is the huge country of China. To the west are the countries of Laos and Cambodia. For hundreds of years, the tiny country of Vietnam was ruled by China. Some things the Vietnamese do are similar to what the Chinese do. But many other things are only Vietnamese.

Vietnamese follow the Chinese calendar, which is based on the moon. A new moon is the beginning of a new month. The holiday of Tet begins on the first day of the new lunar year. This happens sometime between late January and early February. The date is different each year.

Long ago Vietnamese farmers held joyful celebrations and feasts in spring. They wanted to thank the gods for letting the warm season come again. They also prayed that the new crops would be successful. After many years, these early celebrations became Tet, or the New Year.

Tet falls at the same time each year as the Chinese New Year. Like the Chinese, the Vietnamese use an animal to stand for each year. After twelve years, the cycle of animals begins again. The animals that the Vietnamese use for each year are the mouse, the buffalo, the tiger, the cat, the dragon, the snake, the horse, the goat, the monkey, the chicken, the dog, and the pig.

Many people believe that a person born in the year of a certain animal will act in some ways like that animal. For example, a person born in the year of the monkey is thought to be witty, fun loving, and sometimes tricky.

## Getting Ready for Tet

As the time for Tet comes near, Vietnamese Americans hurry to get ready. Everyone celebrates Tet. Many families repaint their homes inside and out. Everything in the kitchen is polished. Each room in the house is cleaned. This helps the house look new. The new look matches the newness of nature, the rebirth of spring.

Some Vietnamese Americans believe that gods live in their homes and protect the family. One of these gods is the kitchen god, or "Ong Tao" (ong-T-ow). An old Vietnamese legend or story says that Ong Tao visits kitchens during Tet to inspect the family's housekeeping. (Many people believe in legends even though they are not always true.)

If Ong Tao finds the house clean, he will give a good report to the Jade Emperor. The Jade Emperor, or king of the heavens, is the ruler of all gods. If the family has a good report, they will have good luck all year. To make certain that this happens, the family leaves out gifts of fruit, honey, and a special fried fish. Ong Tao

During Tet, people often like to watch a play about the kitchen god and the Jade Emperor. These people are hurrying to get a good seat.

will ride back to the home of the gods on the back of the fish. In Vietnamese legends, the fish can become a dragon. So the kitchen god is really riding a dragon to heaven.

Another legend says that the kitchen god reports on the good or bad deeds the family has done the past year. He will also report on the things that have happened in this world since his last visit.

As Tet draws closer, the color red is everywhere. Red is a symbol for good fortune and happiness. (A symbol stands for an idea.) Most homes have New Year's wishes written in black writing on red paper during Tet. The paper, called a scroll, hangs in the living room or above the front door.

Peach blossoms are another symbol of Tet. Everyone smells the sweet smell of peach blossoms. Vases hold branches of blossoms. They are placed on tabletops and shelves. The blossoms stand for the rebirth of spring and a promise of a new beginning.

Peach blossoms are a symbol of Tet. They stand for the rebirth of spring and a promise of a new beginning.

Before Tet arrives, people try to pay all their bills. They do not want to owe any money. Vietnamese Americans believe that if you owe money on the New Year, then you will owe money all year long. People also return anything they have borrowed. During Tet, people try to forget past mistakes and forgive others. It is a new beginning.

Shopping for gifts is another way of getting ready. People love to give gifts on Tet. If the

People love to give gifts on Tet. These statues of Buddha are in front of a Vietnamese store.

family can afford it, children are given new clothes from both their parents and their grandparents.

The children will also receive gifts of money called "li xi" (lee-see). Crisp dollar bills are tucked inside small red envelopes. Even tiny babies are given the small envelopes. Children use this money to buy toys and candy.

This is the busiest time of the year for Vietnamese businesses. Everyone is out buying gifts. Flower shops have customers all day long.

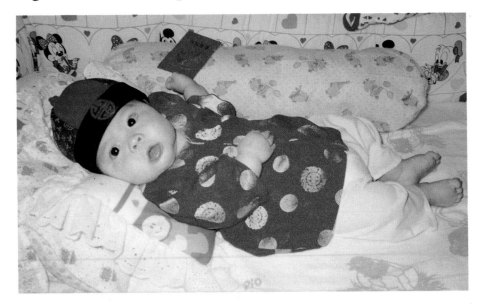

Even tiny babies are given red envelopes on Tet.

Many people buy red gladiolus and yellow Chinese mums to give as gifts. Flowers are a sure sign that Tet is coming.

Food is an important part of Tet. Special foods are cooked before Tet begins. A favorite of everyone is rice cakes, called "banh chung" (bang-chung). The rice cake is wrapped in banana leaves and filled with beans and pork. The cakes have a square shape because Vietnamese once believed that the earth looked

Food is an important part of Tet. These Vietnamese-American children are enjoying traditional food.

that way. Children know Tet is near when they see plates of banh chung on the table.

Dua mon (zua-MON) are pickled radishes, peppers, and other vegetables. These pickled vegetables are usually eaten with banh chung. Mut (uum-UT) is candied dried fruit. It might be a mixture of pineapple, ginger, and coconut. Children love this treat. It is served to guests when they visit on New Year's Day. Every family tries to make special foods and treats for Tet. Everyone wants to make their guests feel happy.

Some Vietnamese Americans like to send New Year's cards. The cards have pictures of apricot or peach blossoms, spring birds, firecrackers, and green rice cakes. The cards wish good luck and happiness for the New Year.

# A Family Holiday

The family is the center of Vietnamese life. Beliefs and customs are passed down from parents to children. (A custom is something that is done over and over again.) The children grow up and pass what they have learned on to their own children.

The most important thing about Tet is that it is a family holiday. Families gather together, sometimes traveling thousands of miles to spend Tet with one another. In recent years, many Vietnamese Americans have traveled to Vietnam for the three-day holiday to spend Tet with family members living there. It is a warm, caring time. If people cannot be with their families, they know that their families are thinking about them. Everyone feels his or her family's love at Tet.

Many Vietnamese believe that the spirits of family members that have died return to earth for the three days of Tet. These family members, who are no longer alive, are called ancestors.

Most Vietnamese have a small altar in their homes for their ancestors. The altar may be a small table or shelf. It is covered with red and gold paper. On the altar, candles and long sticks

Most Vietnamese have a small altar in their homes. This altar has many pictures of ancestors and plates of fruit.

This is an altar in a Buddhist temple. Many family altars also have a small statue of Buddha.

This statue of Buddha is in a garden. Some Vietnamese Americans believe in a religion called Buddhism.

of incense are burned. The incense burns slowly and gives off a sweet-smelling smoke. Often there are pictures of ancestors on the altar.

During Tet, Vietnamese Americans decorate the altars with flowers and fresh fruit. They might also place a cup of tea alongside the food. They pray to their ancestors to protect and guide the family.

An old Vietnamese saying is, "A drop of blood is more important than an ocean of water." This means that families are the most important part of life.

Some Vietnamese Americans believe in a religion called Buddhism. They call themselves Buddhists. The Buddhist religion began in the country of India many centuries ago. It was started by a young prince. His name was Buddha. Many family altars also have a small statue of Buddha.

Some children make hand puppets out of paper bags for Tet.
Dragons are important to the Vietnamese people.

## *School Celebrations*

Some American schools share the excitement of Tet. Teachers talk about the holiday. Boys and girls make scrolls wishing a Happy New Year. Red and yellow streamers decorate the classroom. On the bulletin board are pictures of the animal for the New Year. Sometimes the children learn Vietnamese dances. The favorite dance is the dragon dance. Children also make dragon hand puppets out of paper bags.

Dragons are important to the Vietnamese people. They are called the "Children of the Dragon." An old legend tells a story about a dragon and a fairy princess that fell in love. They married. The wife delivered 100 eggs that later became 100 children. Their children were as brave and kind as the dragon and as beautiful as the princess. The children became the ancestors of the Vietnamese people.

Another legend says that dragons roam the earth during Tet. If you see one, you will have good luck all year long. Children love hearing and reading dragon stories.

Some schools have a Tet party. The children invite their parents. They serve Vietnamese food. Rice is always made. It is easy to cook, and Vietnamese Americans eat rice every day. They might also have noodles, egg rolls, and dried fruit. The parents see the decorations and watch the dances. Everyone eats and has a good time. It is a time for all children to learn some Vietnamese ways.

# The Night Tet Begins

On the night Tet begins, many families attend church or temple. Buddhist families go to the Buddhist temple. The temple has statues of Buddha and is decorated for Tet. In front of a large altar, they pray to their ancestors and to Buddha. They offer up thanks for the past year. They pray that the New Year will be a happy one. They hope their families and friends will be protected and blessed.

Buddhist monks like to give the visitors gifts to bring them good luck in the New Year. The gifts might be mandarin oranges, tangerines, or other fruits, like sugared coconuts or dates.

There is also a box filled with long sticks. The sticks are part of a fortune-telling game.

They look like flat chopsticks. Numbers are written on them. Each number has a special meaning. On the night before the New Year begins, people like to know their fortunes. The people shake the box and let some of the sticks fall out. The numbers on the sticks tell what the person's fortune may be for the coming year.

Then the family returns home. Just before midnight, the father bows before the altar. He

Buddhist temples have statues of Buddha and beautiful decorations.

The night before Tet begins many Vietnamese Americans play a fortune telling game at the Buddhist temple. The numbers on the sticks tell what a person's fortune might be for the next year.

offers food to the ancestors and invites them to join the family. At midnight firecrackers are set off and children beat on drums. It is Tet. A New Year has begun. The family sits down to a big feast with delicious food. They may celebrate all night long.

# *Tet*

The next morning the children receive their red envelopes. Then everyone waits for the first visitor. Many believe the first visitor brings good or bad luck with them. To make sure that the luck is good, the family may invite the first visitor. They will invite someone important and well-liked. It is an honor to be asked to be the first Tet visitor.

The day is spent visiting family and friends. Everyone gives gifts. Some families wrap banh chung in red cellophane to give to visitors. They serve tea and the special treats they have made. Guests bring pickled vegetables and sugared fruit.

Many people believe that what happens on

Li xi (the small red envelopes) hang from this tree. The person who picks the lucky one receives a prize. Children receive li xi filled with money on the morning of Tet.

Tet will be repeated during the coming year. So everyone tries not to argue or say unkind things. Children mind their parents. Parents try not to scold their children. Everyone tries to be polite and nice.

The head of the lion is made from paper and cloth. Everyone enjoys watching the lion dance.

# *Tet Celebrations*

During the three-day holiday, there are always celebrations held in parks or shopping centers. All the Vietnamese Americans in the community come together. This is the time to wish everyone a Happy New Year.

Many of the women and young girls wear special dresses called ao dai (OW-zi). These are long-sleeved silk dresses with high necks. There is a slit up the side. Under the dress, women wear long white silk pants.

Food booths sell banh chung, Vietnamese egg rolls, and thit nuong (tit-NUNG). These are pieces of barbecued meat on a stick. Everywhere there are good smells and special treats.

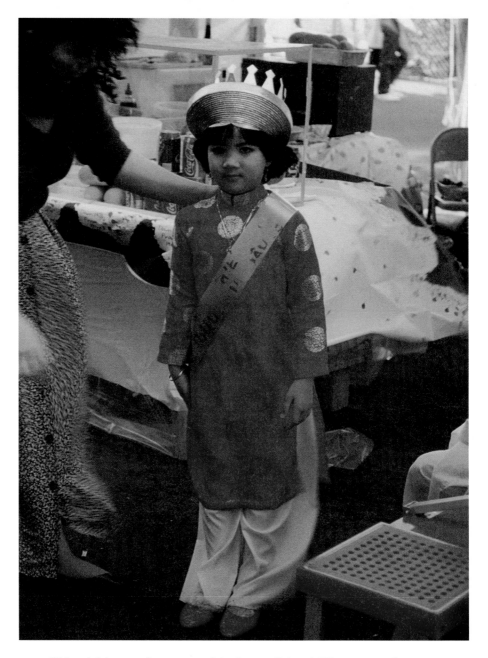

This girl is wearing an ao dai, the traditional Vietnamese dress.

An opening ceremony with flags from the United States and Vietnam begins the celebration. Boy Scouts and Girl Scouts may carry the flags. Then there is a time of silence to remember the ancestors. This is followed by a firecracker show. Hundreds and hundreds of

Food booths sell delicious Vietnamese food.

firecrackers explode. The smell of burnt paper mingles with smoke. The noise is very loud. Many children hold their ears.

Now it is time for the lion dance. The lion's head and long body are made from paper and cloth. Young boys and girls hide under the body. They take turns holding the head and body up. They make the lion move and sway forward and backward. The lion shakes its head and moves to the loud beat of drums. It is hard to watch the lion shaking and moving without laughing.

There are contests for children wearing Vietnamese clothes. From a loud speaker, Vietnamese music plays. Some of the songs are Vietnamese folk songs. Many of the people join in the singing.

After the singing, Vietnamese poetry is recited. Poetry is very important to the Vietnamese. Most people can quote lines of poetry from memory.

There is so much to see and do. There are games of volleyball and other sports. Many people watch martial arts. Another booth has paintings and photographs. Some of the pictures show places and cities in Vietnam. There are also maps. Grandparents or parents show the

There are games of volleyball and other sports at Tet celebrations.

children where the family comes from in Vietnam.

Young girls perform Vietnamese folk dances. Sometimes there are plays in Vietnamese. The favorite one is a New Year's play about the kitchen god. A player wears a purple robe and pretends to be the kitchen god. He makes up funny stories about people. Another person in a red robe plays the Jade Emperor, or king of the heavens. The kitchen god tells the king the made-up stories. The stories make the crowd laugh.

Everyone has a wonderful time. As the Tet celebration comes to an end, Vietnamese Americans are thankful for the past year. There is hope for the New Year. They feel closer to their families and closer to their Vietnamese customs and history. Until next year, "Chuc Mung Nam Moi" (CHOOK MOUNG num MOOEE) or "Happy New Year!"

Boys and girls hide under the body of the lion. They make the lion move and sway.

# *Glossary*

**altar**—A small table or shelf used for religious ceremonies.

**ancestors**—Family members who are no longer alive.

**ao dai**—The traditional Vietnamese dress worn by women and girls.

**banh chung**—Square rice cakes filled with beans and/or pork.

**Buddhism**—A religion founded centuries ago by a young prince named Buddha.

**Chuc Mung Nam Moi**—"Happy New Year" in Vietnamese.

**custom**—Something that is done over and over again.

**dua mon**—Pickled vegetables.

**legend**—A story told over and over. Many people believe in legends even though they are not always true.

**li xi**—Gifts of money tucked into small red envelopes.

**mut**—Candied dried fruit.

**Ong Tao**—The Vietnamese kitchen god.

**temple**—The building where Buddhists pray to Buddha and ancestors.

**thit nuong**—Pieces of barbecued meat on a stick.

# *Note to Parents, Teachers, and Librarians*

To accomodate younger readers, the Vietnamese words in this book have been written without the appropriate diacritical marks. In proper Vietnamese, the words appear as follows:

áo dài

bánh chưng

Chúc Mừng Năm Mới

chữ nôm

Dưa món

lì  xì

mứt

Ông Táo

Tết

thịt nướng

# *Index*